Financial Fables

SEVEN TALES TO TRANSFORM YOUR FINANCIAL LIFE AND MORE

Renee Porter-Medley

Christine Cargnoni

Certified Financial Planner™ Professionals

Special Recognition
Genesis Allione, Illustrator
Marty Wisher, Cover Model
Roberto Briceño, Roberto Photos

Financial Fables™: Seven Tales to Transform Your Life and More
Copyright © 2011 Renee Porter-Medley and Christine Cargnoni
Financial Storytelling, LLC
All rights reserved.
ISBN: 1456360973
ISBN 13: 9781456360979
Library of Congress Control Number: 2010917319
CreateSpace, North Charleston, SC

We dedicate our book to our children, and especially to Christine's son, who was fighting for his life as we struggled to finish this book. We are praying for his continued healing so he can pursue his happily ever after.

Stressful periods, such as this unexpected and heartbreaking medical situation, illustrate why families need to have their finances, and the related areas, under control. The emotional impact steals normal thought processes and a family can easily slip to despair without a stable foundation for support. By taking steps to transform our own lives, we are better prepared to take care of the people we love when they need us.

FOREWORD

All of us want to make the best financial decisions for our families and ourselves every day. But that's not always possible because we may not know enough about financial planning or cannot take the time to learn more about it. Imagine, then, if there was a way to easily and quickly understand the basics of financial planning, and as a result, improve the quality of our lives! Well, there is now—and you don't need to find Aladdin's lamp or be sprinkled with fairy dust to make this wish come true.

Financial Fables, written by two experienced financial planners, recreates fairy tales with a modern twist to give readers of all ages some practical planning tips and sound financial advice. These powerful yet delightful fables are packed with insight and guidance, and they provide practical steps that you can take to achieve financial independence. I highly recommend this book to anyone who wants to take control of the financial aspects of their lives, and for those who wish to share this wisdom with others.

Carolynn Tomin, CFP,® Program Director
Boston University Financial Planning Programs

TABLE OF CONTENTS

INTRODUCTION

Everyone wants a happily ever after. Come with us through the magical land of transformation from frog to prince or princess, from want to comfort, from confused to confident. *Financial Fables* will take us back in time to the stories we were told as children, now told in a different way. These fables help us learn the lessons we really should have learned growing up so that we can make these stories our own—and use them to help reach *our* happily ever after.

The fables presented here offer a fun way to learn some basic principles about financial peace of mind. These fables are short enough to read over a cup of coffee in the morning or as a quick bedtime story. Each fable is followed by seven transformation tips and an opportunity for you to journal about which you would like to apply to your life and which you would like to share with family members or friends. Whether you read one a day or one a week, they will help you create your own happily ever after by helping you make better decisions.

Storytelling is an age-old method of transferring wisdom in such a way that readers or listeners can arrive at their own conclusions—those that fit their own lives, just like all financial plans should. Sharing these fables, and the decisions they help us make, can initiate meaningful conversations that may improve families' financial dynamics.

Like us, you may have wondered why happily ever after is so elusive, even with so many financial how-to books and websites loaded with information and calculators galore. And, like us, you may have realized that wealth does not necessarily mean happiness if other areas of your life are not in balance. That is why many financial planning resources also include direction for life planning.

If you don't know how to make each aspect of financial planning tailor to your own life, then generic websites and books written for the general populous are not going to help. The concepts applied by the characters in the story can be translated to your life. Motivation to be happy can be the determining factor only in that you know what to do when the opportunity to change presents itself.

Many people have told us that everyday duties, and especially their jobs, consume so much of their time that when they finally are free, they just want to have fun. For some, learning financial principles can cure insomnia, very minimally; it is not generally considered to be fun. If that sounds like you, then *Financial Fables* was created with you in mind. Enjoy revisiting the stories of your youth and learning new lessons from old fairy-tale friends—and remember, the moral of these tales is that knowledge, when applied, transforms.

MORAL OF THIS BOOK:

Knowledge applied transforms.

CHAPTER 1

BOOTSY THE CAT

*Once upon a dime, in a financial
tale from not so long ago...*

Feeling the weight of the world on her shoulders after yet another exhausting twelve-hour shift at her job, Diva dragged herself home. Looking down the dimly lit hall to her small apartment, she discovered a scrawny cat spread out flat on her door mat. The dirty, dark cat, with little white feet, had definitely been challenged in more than one fight and small tears in his ears indicated that he'd not come out on the better end of them. Diva looked down at the pitiful creature. *Seriously cat!* She thought, *I am really too tired to deal with you.*

She was already stressed, knowing her parents apparently did not approve of her independent life as a single, thirty-five-year-old woman. They refused to offer her financial help, yet they extended funds to her eldest brother, who was married with an adoring family, and to her younger sister, who still lived with them. Not that Diva begrudged her siblings; she didn't, but being judged for who she was—or who she was trying to be—bothered her a lot. In fact, the beaten-down cat on her doorstep looked like how she felt.

"Little cat, you and I are two of a kind," she told the kitty and no one else.

Since Diva's good heart refused to let her turn away the white-footed black feline, she reluctantly opened the door. The cat sprang to life, mustering just enough energy to scamper inside and once again lie down. Diva named him Bootsy from *Puss in Boots*, because he reminded her of the fairy tale. "Maybe you can help me break this continuous spell of bad luck, little Bootsy," she said.

That night, as Diva checked her e-mail, Bootsy settled right between the keyboard and the monitor. "OK! Another critic," Diva said. But Bootsy just looked at her through the slits of his eyes, turned his head, and fell back asleep.

Much to Diva's dismay, it turned out that Bootsy liked to play in the morning. He woke Diva up early by attacking her feet in bed. Like an alarm clock calling her to life, Bootsy would pounce and pounce until Diva was up and moving. She couldn't even shut him out of her bedroom because Bootsy would cry and whine until she let him back in. But soon, Diva found that waking up early allowed her to get a good start on the day. It gave her time to catch up on the morning news and have a little breakfast.

Another benefit from Bootsy's playful mornings was that Diva could get some much-needed exercise. Soon she started feeling more fit; she looked good, too, which boosted her self-confidence. She found herself wearing a smile to work.

Her friends encouraged her to look for a better job, so she posted her resume on the Internet and started the search. The day of the first interview she dressed casually, but as she reached to drink her last sip of coffee, Bootsy ran between her legs and made her spill it all over herself. "Mischievous cat" she scolded, but then when looking in the mirror she saw that perhaps this job would require a more formal look. So she quickly changed her outfit. Since she didn't get that job, she decided to research how to dress professionally and improve her makeup. *Maybe it was for the best.* She was, for the first time in a long time, taking care of herself. She wanted to show the world that she had value.

And by valuing herself, she thought she could tell a difference in the way that co-workers and family regarded her. Her parents started to invite her for regular dinners with her siblings and their children. The kids started to get to know and adore their Auntie Diva.

Several months of perseverance and numerous interviews rewarded her with a clerical job with normal hours and benefits—including reimbursement for education. She decided on an accredited university that offered online courses. Bootsy continued to sleep between the keyboard and monitor as Diva did her homework, perfectly content to watch Diva and complaining loudly when Diva deviated from their nightly ritual.

After earning her degree, Diva kept learning new skills with the help of personal and professional development websites. One day, when thinking about how far they both had come and how healthy Bootsy had become, Diva thought that a little hat to cover those poor deformed ears would make Bootsy look dashing. When she took Bootsy out, so many people commented on how adorable Bootsy looked that Diva thought she might be able to design a line of clothing for cats.

She decided to form her own business. She took advantage of websites that provided legal, accounting, and business planning information. Eventually, she realized she needed help evaluating and coordinating the advice she had gathered online. Diva hired a financial planner to help her coordinate her personal financial life with her business life. A business friend at a local chamber of commerce meeting warned her that many entrepreneurs put too much of their own wealth back into their businesses.

Diva was thrilled but also overwhelmed by all the information. However, she found that by accomplishing one thing at a time, she could break down an overarching goal into manageable, workable steps. Accomplishments don't happen overnight, like in fairy tales. Diva's success took more than a decade of hard work and dedication.

Just before she turned fifty, Diva was featured in an article in a big business magazine. The article enabled her to share her steps to success and her love for animals.

Diva decided to leave a legacy by making a generous contribution to a foundation for animal welfare and adoption. Bootsy brought such bliss to Diva's life that her heart was filled with joy knowing she would be helping others benefit from an animal friend. As for Bootsy, because of the inspiration he'd provided in those early years, he earned a little diamond-chip collar.

MORAL OF THE STORY:

You can transform your life by taking one step at a time.

DIVA & BOOTSY'S TRANSFORMATION TIPS

1) Decide what to accomplish.
Like Diva, you can decide to take better care of yourself, educate yourself, and find something meaningful in your life.

2) Identify resources.
Like Diva, you can explore online resources and courses to learn new skills.

3) Create a plan.
Diva's plan evolved gradually. Your plan will be an ongoing process. Work at something that you enjoy.

4) Take action.
Diva improved herself physically and professionally.

5) Reevaluate your plan.
Like Diva, you can decide to accomplish more. Diva decided to start her own business.

6) Find trusted advisors.
Like Diva, you can move from website resources to consulting with certified professional advisors in person.

7) Share what you've learned.
Like Diva, you can support a charity that reflects your values.

FACT FROM FICTION:
BOOTSY THE CAT

Heart- warming stories abound about people and their pets. So, it is not unusual to see articles both in the news and on the internet about the way that pets contribute calming effects that lower blood pressure. However, most people are unaware of the Delta Society, an organization that is dedicated to "improving human health through service and therapy animals" according to their website. The Delta Society believes so thoroughly in the therapeutic effects of pets, that it sponsors the Pets Partner® program for volunteers to visit hospitals, rehabilitation and other facilities. A pet is a big responsibility, but the reward appears to be worthwhile. Just ask Diva!

DIVA'S RESOURCES

www.indeed.com or **www.monster.com**
When Diva needed a job, she turned to the Internet to help her find one.

www.beauty.about.com
Diva felt good and wanted the world to see her from the inside out. Take pride in yourself—it's about being happy with your own self-image.

www.shape.com
Diva liked this exercise site. Feeling good about yourself includes your physical well-being, even if that just means a good stretch every day.

www.fastweb.com
Diva wanted some scholarship information, knowing that more education would lead to a better job.

www.womanowned.com
Diva took advantage of grants provided to female entrepreneurs to start her business.

www.startupnation.com
Diva used this entrepreneur site to get information for her startup.

www.pickthebrain.com
Diva needed a little help with her self-confidence. She found helpful articles that made her think about her image on this site.

DIVA'S RECOMMENDED READING

It's More Than Money, It's Your Life!
By Candace Bahr and Ginita Wall

As so many friends before her, Diva found this book easy to read, encouraging, and fun. Diva found chapter 1, "How to Become a Money Star," and chapter 4, "My Brilliant Career," particularly helpful.

MY NEXT STEP:
Diva's story made me realize…

❖ *How much I appreciate…*

❖ *What I have achieved…*

❖ *My opportunities…*

I WILL SHARE THIS FABLE WITH…

❖

CHAPTER 2

LEZZA'S BEAUTY AND HER BEAST

Once upon a dime, in a financial tale from not so long ago...

"Whatever possessed you to spend five hundred dollars on a golf club?" Bellezza raged as color rose in her checks, displaying the anger that vibrated all the way from her toes to her head. She felt more like Beast-Lezza than Belle-Lezza. The fact that her husband just nonchalantly shrugged, feed her emotion as much as the fact that she found out about his purchase when she opened the credit card bill. He hadn't talked to her about it all.

She thought of all the coupon clipping she did each week to make ends meet, while he just went out and blew money like it grew on trees. "Do you think *I like* wearing the same old things, paper bagging my lunch, and getting my hair done on a discounted specials while you live the high life?" He looked at her matter-of-factly. "I just wanted it," he said. "I earn a paycheck, and I have a right to buy something for myself when I want."

She was stunned. They were just not on the same page. But this lack of communication was turning her into a beast, and she didn't like it. She took a deep breath and swallowed her anger. "Whatever," she said. "I guess it is an investment in your golf game, and you usually don't ask for much."

It was true. He didn't go out with the guys to bars, and he also brown bagged it for lunch. But that golf club remained a sore point, especially when Lezza looked at the diamond chips in her wedding ring. She realized that they were practically just kids then, but he had only paid five hundred dollars for it. Of course, she had hinted the past several years that she would like an anniversary ring to commemorate their commitment. *Shouldn't he be saving for one?* Their twenty-fifth wedding anniversary was only three years away. *He doesn't plan ahead,* she fumed.

The next day, the debit card for the joint account was declined on a ten-dollar purchase. *Oh no, there must be a mistake!* Her cell phone was instantly in her hand as she pulled up the bank account on the internet *What?* The balance was $5.65. *OK, How many times have I told him?* Lezza thought. *When he writes checks, he needs to transfer the funds to cover them.* Lezza put back the item she wanted to purchase with a sigh. *How do I put up with him?*

Year after year, she reminded herself that he was a good man, a great father, and a loving husband, so she continued to overlook his financial faults. But now the beast was rising again: *"We are getting older and should be saving for retirement,"* she said to herself. *"He thinks that he's going to work forever and that money is just going to flow in indefinitely."*

After a few days, Lezza calmed down and started thinking about what she could do to plan for retirement. She had not contributed much to her 401(k) program at work. *Just because he doesn't save doesn't mean I can't, she thought. He is not going to change, not after all this time. I have got to do something. We are in our forties and retirement might be twenty years away, but the sooner we get started the better off we will be.*

Lezza attended an educational presentation provided by her 401(k) plan. She learned how money accumulates over time. With an online calculator her plan provided, she figured out that if she had started investing $1,200 per year in her twenties, she would have almost a quarter of a million dollars when she retired at age sixty-seven, assuming the investment earned the historic stock market average annual return of 8 percent.

Lezza also decided that she would set an example by creating a spending plan—what some people call a budget. *Budget is just so negative,* Lezza thought. *It's not that I can't afford to buy items. It's just that I want a plan to spend our money effectively.*

She kept track of what she was spending and asked her husband to use cash instead of credit so he was more aware of what he spent. She noticed that when their expenditures accumulated on credit cards, it could take quite a while to pay them off.

Maybe it's true that he doesn't spend all that much, she thought. There's one way to find out. They set up separate bank accounts—his for his money, hers for hers—and a joint account to which they both contributed to pay their bills. This way, they could be more aware of their personal spending habits.

Lezza also began reading about how money personalities influence the way people spend money and make (or ignore making) other financial decisions. After completing an online questionnaire, she discovered that she had a "coupon clipper" money personality. Unknowingly, she had already taken steps to overcome her financial fears. She realized that by initiating a look at the big picture instead of counting pennies, she could make decisions based upon her values. Her husband would think this might be hogwash, so she completed a questionnaire for him too by asking him questions over dinner. *Hmm all this penny pinching could have had a backlash on him instead of being helpful. It makes him feel in control when he makes a big purchase, the characteristics of a "craver."* She pondered the results of the questionnaire. *It's not an exact science, I guess, and I am not a professional but I think I am on to something.*

Planning for retirement, for him, meant acknowledging that he wasn't a superman. He would have to face a period in his life when he may not be as vital as he was when he was young, and maybe he just would not want to work as hard. She worked on a strategy to get him involved. Lezza started reading more personal finance and wealth-building magazines, but when her husband came into the room she would quickly hide them aside or put them into a drawer. She thought, *Maybe by doing this, I will avoid a conflict and perhaps arouse his curiosity. It worked.* His curiosity eventually got the better of him. "What are you up to?" he asked one day. The opportunity she'd been waiting for arrived. She had been hesitant to tell him because of his attitude but finally she shared information about her decision to contribute more to her 401(k) and receive a matching contribution from her employer

"I want to be able to retire in twenty years with enough money to enjoy myself," she told him. "I want to be able to travel." "Who are you going to be traveling with?" he replied. "Well, if you don't have the money, I guess I'll be traveling with friends. You should be considering the next phase of your life, too!" As soon as the words were out of her mouth, Lezza realized her razor-sharp tongue was cutting too deeply.

Too many times, their arguments had gotten out of control. Hateful words would fly, and they were difficult to recover. She decided to try a different approach that appealed to his craver money personality.

Understanding both their money personalities, she backpedalled to both fit their needs and institute a change in their discussions. She softened her tone. This might be a way to tame the beast and bridge the financial communication gap they experienced.

"Wouldn't it be fun to be able to take a trip to a wonderful new Princeville Golf resort?" she asked. A huge reward for saving might fit the craver need. "Perhaps you might want to consider curbing some of your spending, too, and putting some money into an IRA." He grumbled. Lezza continued, "We have been through too much to give up on a wonderful retirement together. Maybe my coupon clipping has been overboard and a little annoying. I know that probably bothers you as much as your craver attitude toward money bothers me. But we love each other and can work this out." Her husband kissed her and her heart swelled with happiness.

Lezza had tamed the beast and started her transformation. She knew it would be an ongoing process, and at times a challenge. But her marriage, her family, and her happiness, were all worth it. She felt beautiful inside, as if she deserved the name that her parents gave her: Bellezza, the Italian word for beauty.

MORAL OF THE STORY:

Understanding your financial temperament will help you transform.

LEZZA'S TRANSFORMATION TIPS

1) Decide what to accomplish.
Like Lezza, you can decide to focus on what you can control.

2) Explore your resources.
Like Lezza, you can control your own spending and saving.

3) Create a plan.
You can identify the financial decisions you control as Lezza did. She increased her contribution to her 401(k) plan, created a spending plan, and began reading about financial matters.

4) Take action.
Like Lezza, you can start saving for retirement and learn more about investing.

5) Reevaluate.
Lezza recognized it would take time for both her and her husband to transform. Your change may happen gradually also.

6) Find a trusted advisor.

Like Lezza, you may have access to a 401(k) plan administrator for educational materials and meetings.

7) Share.

Like Lezza, you can share what you learn with your spouse and other loved ones. Lezza decided to read about financial matters, starting with books and magazines that she could leave laying about to rouse her husband's curiosity.

FACT FROM FICTION:
LEZZA'S BEAUTY AND HER BEAST

Traditional wisdom indicates that opposites attract in relationships. Lezza and her husband are opposites, Lezza being a coupon-clipper while her husband is a craver. This situation is closer to fact than fiction. One person in the relationship is generally a saver and the other is a spender. Lack of communication about money is one of the causes cited for marriage failure. Lezza and her husband took an important step by creating separate accounts for personal spending. Understanding the difference between want and need is also a big step. Sometimes what appears to be a want is a need, and vice versa. Knowing your own money personality helps you to communicate your wants and needs to your partner.

LEZZA'S RESOURCES:

www.powerpay.org
Lezza needed to manage credit card balances, so she used this site to organize payments to maximize their effect.

www.mint.com
Once Lezza created a spending plan, Mint.com helped her keep track of the cash flow.

www.trueselftruewealth.com
Lezza wanted to understand her spending habits, so she found her financial personality and shared it with her husband.

www.smartaboutmoney.org
Lezza needed a multitude of information to get started in a financial plan.

www.golfdigest.com
Lezza wanted to entice her husband by sharing his interest, and she could find the best golf courses and golf tips on this site.

www.financialcalculator.org
Lezza needed financial calculators to help her make decisions, so she turned to this site to give her the figures.

www.retirementplans.org
With so many different retirement plans, Lezza investigated retirement possibilities.

LEZZA'S RECOMMENDED READING

True Wealth; True Self, a Pathway to Prosperity
By Peter Cole and Daisy Reese

Lezza learned that it is important to understand both her and her husband's financial personalities in order to communicate more effectively about spending and other financial decisions. Marriage, as any partnership, is a two way street.

MY NEXT STEP:
Lezza's story made me realize...

❖ *How much I appreciate...*

❖ *What I have achieved...*

❖ *My opportunities...*

AND THAT I SHOULD SHARE
THIS FABLE WITH...

❖

CHAPTER 3

JACK AND THE BEANS

*Once upon a dime, in a financial tale from
not so long ago…*

Jack hated to see his mother struggling long hours at her
job, and he looked forward to the day he'd be able to
help her. His mother had always encouraged him that he'd
be someone someday. "Hard work and perseverance pays
off" she preached to him. Then she hugged him with the

faith and confidence that only a mother can convey. She just knew Jack would be successful.

She guided him toward a college degree but agreed she would be happy with any advanced education after high school, including a technical school. "Education helps you achieve your goals, plus education can't be stolen from you no matter what happens. With a proper education you can pick yourself up and go on". Not formally educated herself, she spent a lot of time at the public library, where, as she often said, "Information is free and available anytime you want it."

After Jack earned a degree in business at the local university, his mother came to him with the money she had placed in her cow-shaped piggy bank. She asked him to invest the money in a way that would benefit both of them.

Jack knew that being self-employed in a growth business would give him the best return—but starting a business was risky. He was motivated to succeed so he could provide for his mother and himself. Jack continued to do his homework on potential investments. He explored buying a franchise or a business that was already substantially established. He questioned local business owners for feedback for new business in the area. He studied the financial ratios of the past five years and searched the Internet to gauge the demand for various products. After a lot of work, he decided on beans—coffee beans that he would sell with other products in a fabulous shop.

"*What?*" his mother shouted at him. "You invested all the money I gave you on *beans!* Are you out of your mind?" But Jack explained to her how people were willing to pay several dollars for a cup of coffee. He showed her his business plan and how a coffeehouse business could grow, with the right environment.

Jack started his business and managed it well. He offered more promotions and provided higher-quality service to his customers than his competitors. Customers loved the style of Jack's coffeehouse and the homemade food that his mother prepared.

It wasn't long before Jack's investment had grown a hundredfold, and he felt like he had found the goose that laid the golden egg. Then one day, an industry giant discovered Jack's little coffee shop. The giant's representative contacted Jack to buy Jack and his mother's stock in the coffeehouse business and take it over.

When Jack turned him down, the giant became enraged and started to think of ways he could force Jack to sell. The giant's representative claimed that the coffeehouse's golden goose logo was infringing on their trademarks.

Jack hated being coerced, but he also realized that it would be costly to fight the giant. Also, the business had grown too quickly and developed cash flow problems. The small business development center at the local university helped him revise his business plan and apply for a loan, but his coffee shop needed more funds than Jack could afford to borrow to develop to its full potential.

He asked his mother if she would be willing to invest more of her funds in the business but she knew she should stick to her own financial plan and said "No". She needed to keep her investments diversified. So Jack decided to negotiate with the giant after all. Initially, he received free advice from local SCORE volunteers. He learned a lot from these retired executives and business owners who advise budding businesspeople. Then he hired an attorney for legal advice. He decided he would not allow his ego to get in the way of a potentially lucrative business deal.

In the end, Jack and his mother received cash and stock options in the giant company in exchange for their ownership of the coffeehouse. The stock option gave them the right to buy the stock at a lower price with the calculated risk that they would be able to sell the stock higher in the future. They both knew it wasn't wise to keep all of their beans in one basket. They hired a financial planner to help them develop a financial plan and to advise them how, and when, to exercise their options to minimize taxes and maximize returns.

Both Jack and his mother had more free time now that giant controlled the coffee shop, so they decided to volunteer. Jack's mother became active in Junior Achievement, a volunteer organization that teaches business principles to students. Jack decided to volunteer with SCORE. He enjoyed encouraging local entrepreneurs.

Jack's mother also believed so much in education, that she reinvested some of her money in educational software. She hoped that her research would lead her to an excellent return on investment and provide another source of income. Imagine Jack's surprise when he learned that she had made and saved enough money to buy a condominium in the Caribbean for some well-deserved relaxation.

He learned one more lesson: just because children are successful doesn't mean they know everything.

MORAL OF THE STORY

Invest with others, and for yourself, with a plan.

JACK & HIS MOTHER'S TRANSFORMATION TIPS

1) Decide what to accomplish.
Like Jack, you can start with a simple idea and do the research.

2) Identify resources.
Like Jack, you may have a mother or other loved ones who will invest and work with you.

3) Create a plan.
Like Jack's mother, know your limits and stick to your plan.

4) Take action.
Do what you love. The bottom line is that when you work at something you love to do, it is not a chore.

5) Reevaluate.
The business environment changed. Jack reviewed and adjusted his business plan.

6) Find a trusted advisor.
Jack and his mother sought advice from experienced business owners and trusted advisors.

7) Share.

Like Jack and his mother, you can find volunteer opportunities that fit your interests.

FACT FROM FICTION:
JACK AND HIS MOTHER KNOW BEANS

Jack observed that people have seemed to have fallen in love with coffee, but more specifically the place they buy a cup of coffee. He spent time researching coffee beans in order to start his business. The fact is that Starbucks had a very similar start. According to the Starbucks website, Starbucks stock became available to the public on June 26, 1992 at an adjusted cost per share of $.67 – that means that you didn't even have to start your own coffee shop to make a small investment fortune. For example a $1,000 investment in 1992 yielded an investor over $67,000 when the stock, ticket symbol symbol SBUX, traded over $45.00 per share. Far from recommending a purchase of Starbucks stock, this story encourages you to investigate business, as well as investment, ideas.

JACK AND HIS MOTHER'S RESOURCES:

www.ocwconsortium.org
Jack's mother believed in education and used the public library often. Whenever she got a chance, she would select a free course through a university and learn more about a subject.

www.entrepreneur.com
Jack explored resources and information before he decided to be an independent business owner rather than try to buy a franchise.

www.sba.gov
When Jack needed a resource for writing a business plan, he turned to the Small Business Administration's website, particularly the section "Starting and Managing a Business."

www.opportunityfinance.net
Jack found an organization that directs capital to low-income, low-wealth people in order to finance his bean business.

www.helpmywebsite.org
Jack decided that he needed a website and wanted to understand how to build one.

www.ja.org
Jack's mother believed in giving back to the community and helping children achieve their dreams.

www.score.com
Jack utilized the experience of retired business executives who want to help young entrepreneurs by giving them the benefit of their knowledge.

JACK'S RECOMMENDED READING:

The Four Hour Work Week
by Timothy Ferriss

When Jack first started his business, he wanted the business to appear professional but he didn't have a lot of time to devote to marketing. He applied the suggestions in this book to maximize his work time. Other people use this information to become effective in a new approach to work life balance.

MY NEXT STEP:
Jack and his mother's story made me realize…

❖ *How much I appreciate…*

❖ *What I have achieved…*

❖ *My opportunities…*

AND SHARE THIS FABLE WITH…

❖

CHAPTER 4

A WISH FOR RELLA

*Once upon a dime, in a financial tale from
not so long ago...*

Even though it had been several years since Stanley's wife died, he and his daughter Rella still mourned the loss. His business was successful, and he had the financial resources to give Rella everything a girl could want, but he soon realized no amount of material things could replace a mother's love.

Eventually Stanley decided to marry again after meeting a sweet, loving woman to be his wife and mother to Rella. Stanley designed the courtship to include Rella, who sometimes acted as a difficult tween. His new wife knew "It is a package deal" as Stanley would often smile and say to his new spouse. As for Rella, she really did like seeing her father happy again and thought it would be great to have another female to talk to as long as she respected her mother's memory. Stanley was bringing love back not only into his life, but also into Rella's life as well. And for a time, they shared life together and lived harmoniously.

If the tale ended here and everyone lived "happily ever after", it would be wonderful. After all, the family had found a new member that understood their grief with whom they could start life anew. But, Stanley was stubborn about attending yearly medical exams. He just wouldn't spare the time to do it. He would beat his chest and state, "I'm as healthy as a horse". Much to the surprise and shock to everyone, one day, he suffered a heart attack at work. He was rushed to the hospital, where he died.

After the expense of the funeral, his wife cried as she struggled through the pile of bills to pay. Her mind wandered as she tried to figure out where she and Rella stood financially. Stanley had neglected to create a will or any other estate planning documents. When they had spoken about it, he had told her he would get around to it. She hated to push for fear of creating the impression that she had married him for his money, so they never talked about it again. He guffawed, "Nothing is going to happen to me, baby. I am too tough"

She calculated that she and Rella would need to create a strict spending plan because money would be tight. When they married, Stanley had put her name on the home and on the bank accounts. She had the right to survivorship, so she and Rella had a place to live and enough reserves to last for a year or so. However, she had no reoccurring income because Stanley had not created a succession plan for his business. Stanley had owned it with several partners. His share in the business was worth very little by the time the legal matters were settled.

Rella's stepmother received a Social Security benefit because Rella was still a minor child, and her stepmother was able to return to work. These two sources of income were enough to provide for the basics, but extras were not in the budget.

Rella had enjoyed being treated like a princess by her father, and she thought her stepmother was being mean. Over time, her resentment grew. Rella's stepmother had never planned on being a single parent to an unhappy teen, and her resentment grew, too.

By now you may be wondering, "Where is Rella's fairy godmother, and what about the prince?" Yes, Rella did have a fairy godmother—actually, a fairy *grand*mother—who did what she could to bring some fun into Rella's life. We'll get to the prince a little later.

When Rella was a little girl, Fairy Grandmother would buy her special toys and treat her to movies. But now Rella was a teenager, the things she desired were getting pricier. She had asked for an expensive cell phone and a class trip to Europe, and now Rella was dreaming about a car and talking about college. Rella's desires were more than Fairy Grandmother could afford.

One night, on the verge of tears for the loss of her son and the good life for Rella, Fairy Grandmother realized that if she had one wish, she would go back in time and have a very direct conversation with her son.

Sure, wishing for Rella to have a ball at senior prom and a new car for graduation would be more fun, but a long talk with her son to encourage him to create a proper estate plan that would enable him to provide for his family would have a lasting impact.

Because this is a financial fable, Fairy Grandmother's wish was granted. She was granted one more day with her son. and this time, instead of biting her tongue, she said what was on her mind: "Stanley, what if something were to happen to you? How will you be certain Rella and your wife will both be provided for? You have been procrastinating long enough. Today I have one wish, and it's for you to create your will and the rest of your estate plan. I've made appointments for you to visit an attorney, an accountant, and other financial professionals."

Stanley was stunned. How did his mother know about estate planning? He looked at her quizzically, and it struck him that she was right. Not only did Stanley have time to set his affairs in order, he also had the opportunity to say goodbye to his wife and daughter as well as to his mother. By midnight the next day, just as the clock struck twelve, Stanley finished signing the will, implementing the life insurance for his business buy sell, and other important documents.

Of course, when Rella awoke the following morning she didn't remember anything of the twenty four hours with her father. All she knew was that she felt different, more secure. As she went through her day, she realized what it was. She no longer felt resentful. During school, she signed up for the class trip. After school, she went shopping with her friends. Her life seemed carefree again.

Likewise when her stepmother awoke, again with no memory of the past twenty four hours, she felt more content. She no longer caught herself worrying about money. The funds Stanley had left in trust to provide for her and Rella were doing better than ever. She was so thankful he had worked out a buy-sell agreement with his business partners and had purchased life insurance to fund it. There were no legal issues after his death. The resentment created by limited financial resources was gone. Her heart longed for her husband, but she no longer felt the stress of being on her own. She took Rella out for dinner when she returned from the mall, for no apparent reason, just to celebrate life together.

Grandmother's wish had turned into action. She learned that she should talk about financial and related matters with her loved ones. So she shared with Rella the financial lessons she'd learned and encouraged her to begin thinking about how she would build upon the foundation her father had provided. Rella listened to her fairy grandmother, but like most young women, she dreamed of meeting Prince Charming, getting married, and living happily ever after.

So what do you think happens next? How does this story end? Does Rella meet the man of her dreams, who knows the fundamentals of creating and maintaining family finances? Or, blinded by love, does she fall for someone who has fallen in love with her trust money?

Either way, the trust her father put in place had a HEMS clause. HEMS allowed for additional withdrawal for health, education, maintenance, and support. It provided for Rella yet limited excess withdrawals that could put her funds in the hands of a deceitful suitor.

Grandmother was so thankful for her family's second chance that she paid to have their story put in writing and made available through organizations that advise business owners. She never forgot how stunned Stanley was that she knew how to hire advisors, and she made sure the story told readers how to check advisors' credentials and ask the right questions. She hoped the story, titled *What If (Cinder)Rella's Father had an Estate Plan?* would influence others to stop procrastinating.

MORAL OF THE STORY:

Show your loved ones how much you care by putting your will and estate plan in order.

FAIRY GRANDMOTHER'S TRANSFORMATION TIPS

1) Decide what to accomplish.
Like Fairy Grandmother, you can encourage loved ones to create an estate and business succession plan.

2) Explore your resources.
Like Fairy Grandmother, you can influence your loved ones to make better decisions and be frank about the importance of protecting their family.

3) Create a plan.
Like Grandmother, you can introduce trusted advisors to your loved ones.

4) Take action.
Like Fairy Grandmother , you can hold your family members accountable for planning their financial futures.

5) Reevaluate.
Grandmother had a talk with Rella before she met her prince.

6) Find a trusted advisor.

Grandmother sought referrals and checked references to find the right advisors for her son.

7) Share

Grandmother shared Stanley's story with other business owners.

FACT FROM FICTION:
A WISH FOR RELLA

According to the US Census Bureau in a February 2002 Current Population Report by Rose M. Kreider and Jason M. Fields, the median age of widowhood from first marriage was between 50 to 60 years of age, depending upon ethnicity. Although most children are grown by time you reach 55 or so, remember that the statistic is stated as the median age, which means it is the number in the middle. Half of all widows are over that age and half are under that age. Premature death of a loved one causes financial as well as emotional stress. Take steps to make sure that your family survives the impact through a proper will and estate planning documents, and insurances. Insurance protects your family's well-being if you are not available to provide for them yourself.

RELLA'S RESOURCES:

www.publications.usa.gov/USAPubs.php?PubID=5460
Life insurance was an important part of Stanley's business succession plan. It provided funds to cover his family's expenses. A free booklet can be obtained from this website that describes various types of insurance with tips on choosing an agent, a company, and a policy that meet your needs.

www.whyatrust.com
Rella's father also provided specifically for her by placing funds in a trust fund.

www.uslegalforms.com
Because Rella's father loved his family, when he had the chance he prepared a will and other documents so that the legalities of his estate would be more easily settled.

www.agingwithdignity.org
Rella's father died suddenly, but if a longer illness had caused his death, this resource would have helped the family be better prepared. It reviews many options for end-of-life choices and is applicable to people as young as eighteen years of age.

www.charitynavigator.org
Whether it is the Make a Wish Foundation or another charity, Rella can see if dreams come true for others through a legitimate charity.

www.fashiongamesplay.com/makeover
Once Rella's financial resources improved, she could go back to just having fun designing her own fashion makeover by playing the makeover game.

www.life.familyeducation.com
Rella's stepmother needed parenting advice on how to interact more effectively with her stepdaughter.

FAIRY GRANDMOTHER'S RECOMMENDED READING:

Splitting Heirs: Giving Your Money and Things to Your Children Without Ruining Their Lives
By Ron Blue with Jeremy White

Fairy Grandmother was encouraged by the first chapter, "Confessions of Procrastination." It helped her realize Stanley was not the only one who had been putting off creating a will and an estate plan. The rest of the chapters were also easy to read and understand.

MY NEXT STEP:
Rella and Fairy Grandmother's story made me realize…

❖ *How much I appreciate…*

❖ *What I have achieved…*

❖ *My opportunities…*

AND SHARE THIS FABLE WITH…

❖

CHAPTER 5

SNOW WIT AND THE SIX SAVVY DWARVES

Once upon a dime, in a financial tale from not so long ago...

Snow Wit carried her brown leather purse with a certain amount of pride. The smell of the leather along with the large letter D—the designer's insignia—enticed her into a purchase she might otherwise have declined.

She could spend a little more on herself these days, as she had a great fixed income portfolio that she could depend on. More than the purse, she was thankful for the wit and wisdom she had developed over the years.

In her youth, Snow lived under the scrutiny of a wicked stepmother who regarded herself as a queen. How vain, Snow remembered, as the horrible witch of a stepmother spent money hand over fist and put her father in a world of debt. While poor Snow dressed from discount store and re-sell shops, her stepmother never wore anything but the highest end fashion.

While Snow lived in their castle, the queen of the house forced her to work for a pittance. Each day, the stepmother—who valued her physical beauty above all else—stared at herself in her gold-encrusted mirror. Snow had decided at a young age that the risk of staying in the castle was greater than venturing out on her own.

So as soon as Snow turned eighteen years of age, she embarked on her journey into the dark woods of finance with the small amount that she had been able to save. She had read that she should have a financial plan, but the unending complexities and possibilities of putting one together loomed over her, casting a long, ominous shadow. To even think of a long term plan made her cringe. She was taking one step at a time through the dark forest of life. She would run from one website to another, desperately looking for guidance. She needed a safe harbor, a home of her own.

Finally, she stumbled upon a little cottage in the woods. The home belonged to seven little dwarves who worked in a mine each day exploring for new resources. This place looked OK, and she was told she could have room and board in exchange for housekeeping services, so she decided to stay.

The little cottage glowed with warmth and energy. Six of these dwarves were experts at managing different types of risk, and they taught her all they knew. There, she lived happily with the six risk-averse dwarves who protected her—and one dopey dwarf.

The first dwarf was named Stop Loss. He protected Snow from the downside of stock purchases. He taught her that investments cycled up and down over time. Snow had to decide when she bought an investment, how much she was willing to lose before she sold it. Once she decided that a stop loss was needed, she placed the order so that the stock would sell automatically. She evaluated the investments carefully, because she would not want that to happen too many times.

The second dwarf was named Insurance; he guarded against loss from the physical hazards in life. Not only did he protect her health, but also the car she drove, and her very life!

The third dwarf, Reserve Fund, protected her investments by providing a cushion to draw from in a down market. Snow learned that the stock market will fluctuate in periods and it is never good to liquate a solid investment just because the overall market is not doing well. This reserve was her source of cash money to spend during those periods.

The fourth dwarf, Fixed Income, offered Snow a steady cash flow. Snow learned how to earn steady income from dividend paying stocks as well as annuities. Knowing that she had a predictable income made shopping days a little less stressful.

The fifth dwarf, Index, helped her earn long-term growth on her investment that matched the market. She had to decide which index she wanted to follow. She decided on the Dow Jones Industrial Average because it was established in 1896 with a long reputation and represented the diverse thirty corporations in the United States.

The sixth dwarf was named Bonds; he taught her how bonds investment could also provide a consistent source of income. All sorts of entities issued bonds. Local municipalities and government issued bonds when they needed money to improve the community. Most of these bonds were tax free, and Snow liked that the best!

Finally, there was the seventh little dwarf, whom the rest found a bit dopey. All the dwarves wanted Snow to have her heart's desire but only this one encouraged her to spend her money freely and wantonly. Snow quickly learned that spending without reason and proper resources was just a crazy thing to do.

One day, her wicked witch of a stepmother showed up at her door with an apple of an investment. Snow was tempted. The apple was juicy, red and ripe, representing a whole basket full of tips on making and spending money.

Snow bit the apple and started to feel faint.

Luckily, little dwarf Stop Loss was there to help. He sold that stock before it fell too heavily that day. The apple could be a good investment, but not for Snow. It was too volatile for Snow's risk profile. The old witch had set her back once again, but not for much. This time Snow had risk management on her side.

Aggressive investing can be a good thing when it fits a risk-reward profile that's part of an overall financial plan. This was not the only time Snow had gotten a little more aggressive than she should have, but she was happy that Stop Loss kept her from losing more than she could afford.

Snow had also learned to appreciate the Insurance dwarf's FDIC talents that kept her deposits safe within the insured limits. When the Federal Office of the Comptroller of the Currency seized her local bank because of losses due to default mortgages, Snow's account was fully insured.

After biting that darn apple, not only was Snow at risk with her money but also her health. She became ill but her health insurance adequately covered the hospital and doctor's fees.

Some people thought Snow lived a very boring, sleepy life. A handsome prince would complete your happiness, they would tell her. She would just slyly smile in return. In fact, several princes had come along, but Snow wanted to wait for the right one. Besides, she enjoyed her independent financial lifestyle.

She enjoyed managing her investments, and analyzing stocks and bonds. She really understood each investment and why she owned it. In fact, she enjoyed investment research and portfolio management so much that she formed and funded an investment club for girls who were in difficult situations. She wanted to help them the way her dwarves had helped her.

So now, after years of prudent investing and saving, Snow can now buy what she likes, and even splurge on items like that wonderful brown leather purse. In fact, maybe she'll buy the matching leather shoes. Along with a new outfit, it may be just the thing to dazzle the new charming prince in her life.

She chuckled as she thought about how he arrived thinking he would rescue her, but she was already safe and knew she could wait to ride away with him when she was ready—just not yet.

MORAL OF THE STORY:

Manage your risks so you do not have to be rescued.

SNOW WIT'S TRANSFORMATION TIPS

1) Decide what you want to accomplish. Like Snow, you can decide it is time to make a change.

2) Explore your resources.
Like Snow, you can accumulate a small reserve account and make good friends.

3) Create a plan.
Like Snow, you can learn how to protect yourself from different types of risk and how to manage your investments.

4) Take action.
Like Snow, make decisions and learn from your mistakes.

5) Reevaluate.
When Snow could afford to spend, she did so and enjoyed herself.

6) Find a trusted advisor.
Like Snow, you can listen to good advisors and ignore the dopey ones.

7) Share.

Like Snow, you can teach others what you have learned.

FACT FROM FICTION:
SNOW WIT AND THE SIX SAVVY DWARVES

RISK is not a "four letter" word. It is okay to use it regularly in our conversations concerning money, and especially when balancing what the reward is on the other end of the risk. Risk is broadly considered the amount that is willing to be lost in order to obtain a certain gain. A good philosophy to live by, is given in the risk-reward concept that the higher the risk, the higher the potential reward that should be expected. If the reward is not sufficient for the amount of risk taken, automatically consider avoiding the situation. People manage everyday risks by making themselves as knowledgeable about the subject as possible. Some of the knowledge comes from our parents, our friends, and our partners. Everyone has a comfort level in order to sleep soundly at night. Like Snow, make sure you seek and follow the best advice available.

SNOW WIT'S RESOURCES:

www.fdic.gov
Snow could use the information on this site to make sure her bank accounts are insured.

www.trulia.com
Snow Wit was lucky in finding the dwarves' cottage. But she might have used this site if she needed information to determine if renting versus buying a place to live was better. Plus many real estate tips abound.

www.njaes.rutgers.edu/money/investmentrisk.asp
Snow used the information provided by Rutgers University to understand risk and reward concepts.

www.morningstar.com
Snow learned about different funds and investment styles when she reviewed the equity allocation in her portfolio.

www.quantumonline.com
The fixed income part Snow's portfolio includes certificates of deposit, bonds, possibly annuities, and dividend-paying stocks. Snow liked to check this site for dividend-paying stocks. She always reviewed the fixed income allocation in her portfolio.

www.treasurydirect.gov
Snow used this website to learn about treasury bonds and how to purchase them directly from the government.

www.healthinsurance.org
When Snow got sick from the apple, part of her risk protection was having adequate health insurance.

SNOW'S RECOMMENDED READING:

Investing for the Utterly Confused
By Paul Petillo

Snow was confused when she started her journey into financial freedom. She was encouraged by the author's analogy that investing is like learning how to drive—you don't just hop in and take off. Also, chapter 4, which discusses risk, was particularly helpful. It reinforced the lessons learned from the risk-averse dwarves. This book along with other research helped her develop an investment plan that fit into her overall financial plan.

MY NEXT STEP
Snow's story made me realize...

❖ How much I appreciate...

❖ What I have achieved...

❖ My opportunities...

AND SHARE THIS FABLE WITH...

❖

CHAPTER 6

LITTLE RED AND GRANDMOTHER HOOD

*Once upon a dime, in a financial tale
from not so long ago...*

A beautiful young town maiden fell deeply in love with the local woodcutter and they married. The two created a world of their own with a lovely home deep in the woods, where he worked, and they hoped to raise a large family. Alas, the couple was blessed with one son but when he reached adulthood, he moved from the woods for a new job.

The son and his wife had a daughter. Now the once-young maiden was a grandmother. Grandmother made her granddaughter a flowing red cape to wear so she could walk through the woods to visit without a hunter mistaking her for an animal. The local townspeople became accustomed to seeing her walking the path to the house in the woods, and affectionately called her Red.

Then, one day tragedy struck. The woodcutter was splitting logs when his heart failed. When her husband died, Grandmother could not bear to move from their home. She did not feel alone there because she was surrounded by the memories of her family in the house she had shared with her husband.

Yet, being on your own after a lifetime with a partner is never easy. But since she had established a circle of friends through her church community, she was never in want of company. When she desired some social time, she would hop into her four-wheel drive and head into town without hesitation.

After a number of years passed, however, she could no longer navigate the narrow, tree-lined country roads, especially at night. As she aged, so did many of her friends, who had the same problems driving. Being off the beaten path was now a definite disadvantage. For the first time in her life, she was feeling rather lonely.

Fortunately, her sweet granddaughter came to visit her every week. She looked forward to seeing the young girl who still wore a flowing red cape. Yet, Grandmother also worried about Red because the woods could be a dangerous place in which to travel. If anything were to happen, she would feel so responsible. Whenever Red was running late, she started imagining that Red was in trouble and there was nothing she could do to help.

Red looked forward to her weekly visits with Grandmother and wished she could go more often, but school, work, and her other commitments kept her very busy. She looked forward to the day she could afford to take care of Grandmother, if only she could persuade her to leave the woods. She didn't know if Grandmother was telling her the truth about staying in the woods because of memories. Red wondered if it was really about money, but she didn't want to discuss it because she didn't want Grandmother to think she was prying into her business.

Grandmother had good reason to be alert to danger because a big, bad wolf was stalking her and Red, watching their pattern of activity. Now that Red was grown, he could see that she would be absent from time to time. He kept track of Red by the GPS system on her new smart phone.

Red was unaware that her smart phone could record her location.

The wolf took advantage of her absence one day and telephoned Grandmother. "Mrs. Hood," he said, "I am sorry to report that security at the XYZ store is holding Red because she did not pay for an item. I am sure it is a mistake, and can be corrected. If you could give me a credit card number we can rectify the situation without calling the police." Grandmother hurriedly grabbed her purse, without thinking that she should check the caller's veracity with a return telephone call. But as you might have guessed, the charge did not go through for a five-dollar lipstick, as the caller had indicated. Rather, the charge was for twenty-five hundred dollars.

By the time Grandmother had gotten in touch with Red, the money had been collected and transferred to the end party.

Her family criticized Grandmother in acting so hastily to give out her credit card over the telephone and falling for a scam. Grandmother defended herself, saying that she would do whatever it took to keep Red safe. " I couldn't take the chance that she might actually had been in custody. An arrest, even if it was a misunderstanding would hurt her record, and maybe hurt her chance to get a good job!" She balked—she was not a child and it was her money.

The family decided that it was best to keep it a secret so that the townspeople did not know Grandmother had been tricked, since they deemed it so embarrassing. They worried that people would think Grandmother was no longer fit to live alone. After all, the credit card company had insurance, and the money was credited back to Grandmother's account.

Trying to keep the scam a secret was a mistake, however. The first wolf sold Grandmother's information to a more sophisticated, bigger, bad wolf.

One day, a clean-cut, charismatic wolf of a young man knocked on Grandmother's door. Grandmother knew she could size this caller up in person, and she could tell he was a nice young man. The bad wolf smiled sweetly and said he worked for Home Alone No More Advisory Company. She had won a free gift and, by the way, he would like to tell her about a plan that would increase her income with no risk to her principle, provide all the funds she needed for long-term care when needed, and there would still be a nice little inheritance for her family. *Yes!* This was one simple, safe investment that would address all of her concerns with no risk, he cajoled.

Grandmother found herself relieved to find a way to address all of her concerns, and she was ready to sign up for the account when Red walked in the door. As the wolf of a salesman began to explain the account to Red, she exclaimed, "Grandmother, shouldn't you establish a plan first? How do you know you really need this account?"

The wolf smiled sweetly, and responded, "Of course, my dear. Her plan is right here on my laptop. Come closer so you can see it better." Red looked at the report; it showed Grandmother's proposed account increasing in value and generating significant income.

Red had no idea Grandmother had accumulated so much money. "Grandmother, shouldn't you have a variety of investments?" she asked. "I've heard that you shouldn't keep all your eggs in one basket."

The wolf smiled sweetly and said, "Of course, my dear. Listen to these testimonials recorded on my laptop. Come closer so you can hear them better." Red listened and was impressed as the women on the recording described their newfound peace of mind.

"Grandmother, I had no idea you were worried about care," Red said. "But shouldn't you be talking to me first instead of this salesman? After all, I have always planned on taking care of you some day."

The wolf smiled sweetly and responded, "Of course, my dear. Family members should care about each other, but they shouldn't have to care for or become a burden to each other. Let me tell you about how time-consuming and expensive care can be. I am sure you are a busy girl, and it could really take a bite out your inheritance if Grandmother spent her money on care."

This all sounded too good to be true, and for a moment Red thought about checking out the wolf and his firm with her state's Department of Financial Services and perhaps the Senior Protection Agency. But Red was as captivated by the wolf as Grandmother, and she didn't express any more concerns.

The wolf from Home Alone No More Advisory firm had them both tied up. He quickly signed up Grandmother for the one account that supposedly addressed all her concerns.

The next week, as Red was walking through the woods to Grandmother's house, in the distance she spotted Gary, the woodcutter, working a little beyond the trail. Gary looked after Grandmother as he had taken the woodcutter position when Grandpa Hood had passed away. He liked to keep an eye out for Red too, but for a different reason.

"There's a wolf in the woods", he called over to Red as she was passing by. Red stopped abruptly and walked towards Gary, who proceeded to warn Red about the wolf that had been to his mother's home last week. He told her that the wolf was charming and the account he was selling was appealing, but it was not the best alternative for his mother. Gary also reminded Red that it is not prudent to persuade someone to put most or all of his or her money into one type of account, as his mother had done. In addition, Gary had researched the company the wolf worked for and the account he was selling. The woodcutter discovered it was the most expensive and restrictive account of its type, and a number of complaints had been filed with the state about the "free" gift sales tactic. Receiving gifts helps to break down barriers and causes people to ignore their better judgment. Also, the way this account was promoted led many seniors to make a major decision without properly planning and reviewing alternative recommendations.

Red told the woodcutter that it was too late. Her grandmother had already opened the account. The woodcutter responded, "No, it is not too late. Read the contract. Your grandmother has thirty days to change her mind. If you need help, I will apprehend the wolf for you and tell him to cancel the agreements and return your grandmother's money."

Both Grandmother and Red accepted and appreciated the woodcutter's help. They were too embarrassed to call the wolf themselves. They wondered how this could have happened to them. How did they get so caught up by this presentation? Finally, they started to talk with each other about money and related issues for the first time.

Grandmother confessed her concerns about care, and that she did not want to be alone any longer. Also, it seemed to her that she that had plenty of money, but then again she wasn't 100 percent sure it would last as long as she might live. She often wondered if she could afford to help Red out now so Red could work less and concentrate on school more. It seemed silly to worry about leaving Red an inheritance years from now when it seemed as if Red could really use some financial help now. Plus, she had always wanted to establish a little scholarship fund at the school for woodcutters in memory of her late husband. Both she and her husband had been raised to be secretive about finances, so she never thought to talk to Red about any of this until now.

Red acknowledged that she was busy, sometimes too busy. Even though she knew better, she had accepted what appeared to be an easy solution to what she thought was Grandmother's concern. She thought Grandmother just wanted to earn a higher interest rate to generate more income. Also, she'd thought that Grandmother understood what she was doing—and, after all, it was her money.

Gary, the woodcutter, stayed for a little while sharing what he had learned from assisting his mother: "First, we scheduled a meeting with a Certified Financial Planner, who asked my mother what she would like to accomplish with her money, how she would like to be cared for if the need arose, and if she would like to provide for her family and any charitable organizations. Then the financial planner developed and presented her with a written plan that met my mother's unique needs, and provided her with recommendations and alternatives to think over."

Red and Grandmother recognized that this was just what they needed to do, too. They decided to interview Gary's Certified Financial Planner and they used an online planner search to identify two others. They also found some great resources on their state's Department of Financial Services website, including fraud alerts.

Red and Grandmother reached a new stage in their relationship. They recognized the benefits of becoming comfortable talking about money and getting the professional advice they both needed. Red was able to admit she really could use some financial help now, and Grandmother decided to formalize a long-term care plan so they would both be prepared if the need arose in the future.

Finally, after they both experienced how easily they could be persuaded to do something when it sounded so good, they agreed to check in with each more often and seek independent input before making major decisions.

A year or so later, Red was able to finish school debt free with Grandmother's help. Grandmother established the scholarship fund that was once only a dream. She also became a spokesperson for the state agency for seniors and hired a companion to drive her to her appointments. Grandmother was out of the woods now more than ever, and was enjoying one more round of happily ever after— and Red was well on her way to hers. Grandmother also decided to move from her home. It was time for a new young maiden and her husband to raise a family in the woods.

MORAL OF THE STORY

Families that plan together, stay safe together.

RED AND GRANDMOTHER HOOD'S
TRANSFORMATION TIPS

1) Decide what to accomplish.
Grandmother wanted to live in the woods, but not be stuck in the woods. Also, she wanted to be sure her money would last as long as she lived, and she wanted to help Red and others.

2) Explore resources.
Red and Grandmother talked with a friend who had been in a similar situation.

3) Create a plan.
Grandmother Hood started a financial plan by visiting the federal government site, www.MyMoney.gov. Then she hired a certified planner to further help her develop a written financial plan.

4) Take action.
Red and Grandmother began communicating openly about money and care. Grandmother implemented her financial plan.

5) Reevaluate.
Grandmother realized she had let herself get stuck in the woods and become vulnerable, so she

found a way to get out and get active. You can take an active role in deciding your living style.

6) Find a trusted advisor.

Grandmother considered a recommendation from a friend but also researched two others from websites for professional organizations.

7) Share.

Like Grandmother, you could be generous and create or support a scholarship fund that will help your grandchildren and other children, too.

FACT FROM FICTION:
LITTLE RED AND GRANDMOTHER HOOD

Grandma Hood was lucky that she had the woodcutter to protect her from the big bad wolf. But those of us that do not have a woodcutter handy might want to turn to The Federal Trade Commission, whose motto touts "Protecting America's Consumers". The FTC teaches to defend, deter, and detect identity fraud. (www.ftc.gov – Quick Finder Heading: " Identity Theft" or telephone (202) 326-2222) Unfortunately, some identity fraud can occur even before a child is born, if a social security number that is in part based upon the year that the child is born can be generated by a fraudster. It is important to check the major credit agencies even for children, so Grandmother Hood should encourage Red to check her credit report as well as checking her own. Receive one free credit report per year at www.annualcreditreport.com.

RED AND GRANDMOTHER HOOD'S RESOURCES:

www.nefe.org or **www.smartaboutmoney.org**
One of the best websites for personal financial information is sponsored by the National Endowment for Financial Education.

apps.finra.org/Investor_Information/Calculators/1/RetirementCalc.aspx
Grandmother used this calculator to estimate if she would have enough funds to see her through her retirement years. This regulatory organization also provided Grandmother with tips for older investors on its "Protect Yourself" page.

www.longtermcare.gov
Grandmother Hood and Red should have reviewed a long-term care plan and how much it would cost.

www.idtheftcenter.org
Grandmother Hood could also have turned to this non-profit organization to report identity theft.

www.iii.org
Grandmother and Red Hood found information about annuities and other insurance products through the Insurance Information Institute.

www.ncea.aoa.gov
When Grandmother Hood began to help others, she directs them to the National Center on Elder Abuse which included information on adult protective services.

www.wiredsafety.org
Red and Grandmother incorporated Internet and mobile phone safety into their routines to protect themselves.

GRANDMA HOOD'S RECOMMENDED READING:
The Shell Seekers
By Rosamunde Pilcher

Grandma liked the story of a strong woman taking control of what she would provide for an inheritance. She considered herself lucky that she had Red for a granddaughter, but knew that sometimes "family" can include good and true friends, too.

MY NEXT STEP

Red and Grandmother Hood's story made me realize…

❖ How much I appreciate…

❖ What I have achieved…

❖ My opportunities…

AND SHARE THIS FABLE WITH…

❖

CHAPTER 7

SLEEPING BEAUTY WAKES UP

Once upon a dime, in a financial tale from not so long ago...

A baby girl was born that was so beautiful, her parents were reminded of the beauty reflected in the dawn of a new day. That was the reason they named her Aurora. With her soft skin, dainty figure, and sharp mind, anyone who saw Aurora would think that things came naturally to her. And they were right. Her generous nature and charisma caused people to go out of their way for Aurora, because they enjoyed seeing her friendly smile.

Aurora's parents had it all figured out. They selected the right schools and activities that enabled her to get into the right college and start an impressive career after graduation. They made her a princess in all the ways they could and worked hard to remove anything from her path that would get in the way.

For many years, everything did go according to plan. After college Aurora began a great career and married her prince. Aurora and her husband enjoyed a nice lifestyle funded by two incomes. They were able to spend freely. They bought a spacious house and had two adorable children.

Then, one day, things started going wrong. Things were going so wrong that Aurora wondered if someone had put a curse on her. Aurora's husband lost his job due to cutbacks at his corporation. "Oh, don't worry," Aurora said to him, "this is just a temporary setback, you will find even a better job, you are so talented". She was so confident everything would be fine that they did not cut back on their spending. However, Aurora's income was not enough to cover all their expenses. They began tapping into their savings. Eventually, they began using credit cards to make up the difference. They only used credit cards for necessities like groceries and medical expenses, but over time they went deeply into debt. Debts grew like thorny weeds that soon became large bushes and started to choke them financially.

They had never experienced such a difficult economic climate, so they did not recognize the severity of their situation. They had a rude awakening when their accounts were turned over to a collection agency and the calls started. Aurora's dream like life had become a nightmare.

Aurora thought it would be appropriate to ask her parents for help paying off the debt. Of course, she was a little embarrassed, but she did not know where else to turn. She had come across a statistic that nearly 60 percent of parents provide for, or have provided, financial support for their adult children even when they were no longer in school. She thought, *Why wouldn't her parents want to help her?*

However, Aurora's parents had spent so much raising and educating Aurora that they only had just enough funds left to meet their own retirement needs. They tried to provide some advice, but found they felt too guilty to be effective. They wondered if they were somehow to blame. Perhaps they should have better prepared Aurora for events like this rather than sheltering her. Aurora was shocked, her parents had never said no to her before.

Aurora did not know where else to go for help, and she began wondering if they should declare bankruptcy and just let the house go into foreclosure. Around this time, her fairy godmother telephoned and asked if she could come for a visit. *Why not*, thought Aurora, *someone should enjoy this house before we lose it.*

Once she arrived, Fairy Godmother knew something was wrong and asked how she could help. Aura explained and Fairy Godmother pondered the situation, "Hmm" said Fairy Godmother, "I can't remove the financial difficulties with the wave of a wand, and I am not sure I would even if I could. I highly recommend that you and your husband attend a class that I know will help you get out of debt and on the path to financial freedom. Financial Peace University was the answer for me, but you can check out similar classes from other organizations." Fairy Godmother offered to pay the small (less than one hundred dollars) registration fee as her way of helping Aurora. She also offered to babysit so Aurora and her husband could attend class together.

After the first class, Aurora and her husband began feeling hopeful. The instructors were encouraging. The books and other resources were just what they needed. For the first time ever they were communicating in a meaningful way about family finances. After just a few classes, they recognized that much of their spending was on things that were nice but not necessary. They learned ways to control spending by comparing the price versus the value of a purchase. Although overdue bills and long term debt reared it's ugly head, Aurora and her husband were now ready to fight it, cut it into pieces, and to live victoriously. By the end of the course, Aurora and her husband had a plan that would keep them in their home and out of bankruptcy.

Aurora's eyes were now open to the wide range of free financial planning resources. She regularly visited websites to find information, and took advantage of online calculators to help her make better decisions. Some websites even provided free counseling services that helped her understand more difficult topics, like getting out of debt.

Aurora and her husband found they enjoyed discussing articles and books about family finances and, most importantly, being able to follow some of their suggestions.

One of the best suggestions was how to give children the gift of financial wisdom. They decided not to shelter their children from financial realities. Rather, they included them in financial conversations, when appropriate, and found kid-friendly websites and books that taught valuable lessons about money.

These family conversations really made the difference when Aurora's husband found a job and they had two incomes once again. Instead of spending more, they decided to replenish their emergency fund and start a family investment club as a way of saving for their children's college expenses.

Aurora and her family grew to understand that long-term unemployment is just one of many unexpected life events that can occur. What seemed like a curse at first had become the catalyst that not only helped them to gain their own financial freedom, but also to become advocates of developing a spending plan and avoiding debt. They also reaped the rewards of learning about the entire financial planning process. Eventually, Aurora and her husband wanted to give back, so they volunteered to be facilitators of the financial class that had impacted their lives. They scheduled several sessions a year in their community so they could help other families wake up and avoid debt and other financial problems.

They were thrilled to help others achieve their happily every after.

MORAL OF THE STORY:

Life happens; don't give up when your plan does not work out. Get help.

AURORA'S TRANSFORMATION TIPS

1) Decide what to accomplish.
Like Aurora and her husband, you can decide to deal with your financial troubles rather than give up.

2) Explore the resources.
Like Aurora and her husband, you can take a recommended class, explore websites, and read books.

3) Create a plan.
Aurora and her husband decided to discuss and follow the advice from the class.

4) Take Action.
Like Aurora and her husband, you can continue to apply what you learn.

5) Reevaluate.
Like Aurora and her husband, you can adjust your lifestyle expectations.

6) Find a trusted advisor.
Like Aurora and her husband, you can take advantage of free counseling.

7) Share.

Like Aurora and her husband, you can teach others, including children, what you learn.

FACT FROM FICTION: SLEEPING BEAUTY WAKES UP

Personal bankruptcies are complex and an individual should consult an attorney if considering bankruptcy. Two of the options available under Title 11 of the United States Code are Chapter 7 and Chapter 13. Both options would result in negative ratings on the individual's credit report. Since the negative ratings could be harmful to future credit, if possible, it may be better to sell assets and reassess your spending plan before considering bankruptcy like Aurora and her husband. Some individuals that experienced the crash of real estate values struggled with "underwater" mortgages – which means that they owed more money on their homes than the home's new value. Refinancing to a lower interest rate has helped some borrowers to make lower payments. The difference between the old and the new payment provides more available cash that can be put to an investment account. The resulting investment will help overall financial recovery even if the house itself as an asset does not regain its previous value.

AURORA'S RESOURCES:

www.daveramsey.com
Fairy Godmother found Financial Peace University to be helpful to her. She recommends it as people of all ages claim to have benefitted from this class.

www.crown.org
Aurora and her husband connected with an informative Money Map coach who helped them learn how to use biblical wisdom and the financial tools available on the CROWN website.

www.nfcc.org
Aurora found a lot of great information and calculators on the National Foundation for Credit Counseling website. The website also explained how to connect with the NFCC's free or low-cost credit counseling services.

www.feedingamerica.org
If Aurora and her husband had not been able to stabilize their financial life, this national network of food banks would provide assistance. " Every food recipient is treated with dignity and respect. The call is free. The food is free".

www.pricegrabber.com
Aurora started to compare the price of items she was considering purchasing.

www.spendster.org
Aurora learned from the stories on this site. They address compulsive and wasteful spending in a lighthearted but impactful way.

www.kids.gov
Aurora and her husband found kid friendly online learning activities and games starting for kindergarten age and up.

AURORA'S RECOMMENDED READING (ONE BOOK THAT HELPED HER AND ONE THAT HELPED HER EDUCATE HER CHILDREN):

Make Money Not Excuses
By Jean Chatzky

This no-nonsense book helped Aurora and her husband "wake up and take charge," as Jean Chatzky so bluntly puts it in her opening paragraph.

AND

Raising Money Smart Kids: What They Need to Know About Money and How to Tell Them
By Janet Bonder

The author is upfront about her own successes and failures. She shares advice that has been used successfully by some parents, even if it did not work for her.

MY NEXT STEP

Aurora's story made me realize...

❖ How much I appreciate...

❖ What I have achieved...

❖ My opportunities...

AND SHARE THIS FABLE WITH...

❖

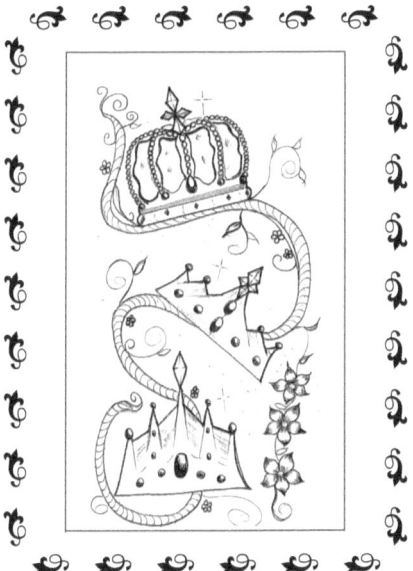

A WICKED SPELL IS BROKEN

A true tale from not so long ago...

The queen was blessed with three sons, princes who were the joy of her heart. Each prince exhibited a great, individual quality. The oldest prince had great knowledge, the middle prince was charming, and the youngest prince was wise. One ordinary day, without warning, Prince Wise was stricken by an evil spell and carried away.

After arriving at the hospital, the prince was still somewhat conscious, but then seizures began, and the virus that infected his brain just would not stop. He continuously seized, and there was nothing that could be done to break the spell other than to put him into a deep sleep.

The first days were hopeful. The queen and the other two princes were certain the spell could be broken. All they had to do was figure out the cause. "Just what was this curse that afflicted him?" they asked. "Is it Rocky Mountain spotted fever? Is it West Nile virus?" No one knew the answer. More tests were required. Spinal taps were performed. But when all the tests had been performed, still no one knew what caused the spell, and they could not break it.

Months passed, days with blank hope that today would be the day he awoke, came and went. All activities in the kingdom revolved around holding him in this world. Nothing else was important. The Queen and Prince Wise's brothers attended his sleeping body. Someone stayed with him every day. They read to the prince, held his hands, and continuously hoped that Prince Wise felt their message of love and that he knew they were there. Their hearts were united, and every Friday called upon everyone in their kingdom to pray for Prince Wise.

Day in and day out, Prince Wise's brothers searched for a way to break the spell, and they supported the queen in her distress. They were stunned when one day, the wizards in the white coats came to tell the queen that nothing more could be done for him at the this hospital. Even if Prince Wise woke now, he may not be able to think or move on his on his own, "Be reasonable," one wizard suggested. "Would he want to live this way? Maybe he should be released from the spell through death." But the queen reasoned that if she was given a chance to fight this spell, fight it she would.

She gathered all her strength. She used everything at her disposal, including—and most importantly—insurance information. She telephoned one insurance representative after another trying to get approval to transfer the prince to a faraway kingdom that would try once again to wake up him up. She recognized that the new wizards were the last chance to save Prince Wise. Thankfully, the new wizard had agreed to try to break the spell, so the prince was loaded onto a flying dragon and taken to the new land. The queen and her sons had to travel to be with the prince; it was a difficult journey, but the queen deemed it necessary, and the princes complied.

This new wizard was impressed. "Never have I seen siblings so involved in breaking a spell, so willing to battle in this manner," marveled the people of the new land. The brothers were exhausted, but they continued to support their mother in her decision to keep fighting.

After many months, the spirit of the Christmas holiday was upon them, and although they continued to provide for others in the kingdom, there was little cheer in the hearts of the queen and her sons. The young prince's body had started to shut down from the long, deep sleep. Little by little, he was slipping away from their grasp, but they continued their vigil over his still body.

Thankfully, Christmas is still a time for miracles. Four days before Christmas, Prince Wise opened his eyes and saw Prince Knowledge sitting across the room. He couldn't move even a single finger or a toe. All he could do to communicate was blink his eyes. In months to come, young Prince Wise proved the other wizards wrong. He had survived the deep sleep with his mind intact; he just needed to learn to move his body again.

This tale truly has a happy ending. Prince Wise continues to improve with his rehabilitation. Prince Knowledge was able to complete his doctorate, and Prince Charming was able to seek his fortunes in a new kingdom. When asked about their good fortune the princes share the blessings that were so much more certain than wishes could ever be. The first two are faith and a loving family; both of these treasures were built up over time by reliance on prayer and making each other a priority. The third blessing was having made the financial decision to purchase medical insurance a priority. Without it, Prince Wise would surely have died. The new hospital had flatly refused to even look for a bed for him without the proper insurance.

The royal family is so thankful the queen had been applying financial planning knowledge to their kingdom for many years. Not only had she managed risk by purchasing medical insurance, she had accumulated adequate cash reserves and had purchased investments that were able to generate income when the family needed it most. Following these and other sound planning principles were essential to her ability to support herself and her princes during a major medical crisis.

MORAL OF THE STORY:

Hope and plan for the best, but always be prepared for the worst.

REFLECTION
The story about the wicked spell made me realize...

❖ *How much I appreciate...*

❖ *What I have achieved...*

❖ *My opportunities...*

AND SHARE THIS FABLE WITH...

❖

TRANSFORMATION

Fables and fairy tales traditionally teach important lessons.

We hope the seven financial fables in this book show that seldom do people live happily ever after without some effort on their part.

We hope you are inspired to make the effort. Each of these fables describes different financial situations. Perhaps you will recognize yourself in one of them and discover the tips that will help you transform your financial life. Consider reading the tales more than once to take something different from them each time.

We may get started with one small step at a time the way Diva did with Bootsy's help. Lezza demonstrates that it is never too late to change, and that other people in our lives are very important in our financial decisions. Jack and his mother take us down the road of investment and business. Rella's story tells us we need to protect and plan for our loved ones now while we are able. Snow Wit teaches about the reward of managing risk through her journey with the protective dwarves.

Each story builds upon the other—until plans go awry for Red and Grandmother Hood as well as for Aurora, our sleeping beauty. However, they all encourage us to recover and continue the journey to our happily ever after.

Each tale has seven tips that follow a familiar pattern: (1) decide what you want to accomplish; (2) explore your resources; (3) create a plan; (4) take action; (5) reevaluate; (6) find trusted advisors; and (7) share.

Financial stability is an important part of the foundation from which people can grow to self-actualization—in other words, transform themselves into who they were meant to be. Financial stability is defined differently for different people, and that is why financial plans are seldom one-size-fits-all packages.

Some people who have modest incomes and savings have a plan that enables them to feel perfectly comfortable with their lives and happily proceed to accomplish their goals. On the other hand, some people with millions of dollars have a difficult time making ends meet.

Many reports exist of lottery winners, entertainment stars, professional athletes, and others who have gained tremendous monetary wealth, then lost it. In contrast, stories exist of hourly and salaried employees who never really flashed much wealth in their lifetimes, but left a huge legacy to a college or charity.

No matter your income level, whether you have a little or a lot of money, you can transform into a princess or prince who truly rules their financial kingdom.

REMEMBER THE MORAL OF THIS BOOK:

Knowledge applied transforms.

PEOPLE WHO
HELP WISHES
COME TRUE

Some of our financial fable friends have the time to take advantage of online and other resources, but others found it helpful to meet with advisors in person. Good advisors can be a lot like fairy godparents who help you make your wishes come true. Here are some websites you can visit to search for an advisor and find a wide range of helpful resources.

To find a Certified Financial Planner, visit the websites for the Certified Financial Planner Board of Standards and the Financial Planning Association.(FPA) Both of these organizations will help you learn about financial planning, how to choose a planner, and how planners are licensed and compensated.

The FPA site (**www.fpanet.org)** provides webinars and other resources on topics such as budgeting and estate planning.

The CFP site (**www.cfp.net**) provides the opportunity to order a free financial planning kit and download the *Consumer Guide to (Financial) Self-Defense.* Start your plan and find more resources on the CFP site. (**www.letsmakeaplan.org**)

To find a Certified Public Accountant, visit the American Association of Certified Public Accountants' website at **www.aicpa.org.** For resources to inform children, teens, parents, military members, and business owners about financial issues, visit the website created by the AICPA to assist the public, (**www.360financialliteracy.org**).

One way to find a licensed attorney is to visit the American Bar Association's website (**www. findlegalhelp.org)**, which was created to help the public find legal help. This site also provides information about your legal rights, hiring an attorney, and even self-help resources.

To learn about investing and how to increase your financial knowledge, visit the Financial Industry Regulatory Authority's (FINRA) website, (**www.finra.org),** and the Investors Protection Trust **(www.investorprotection.org)** Both these websites provides articles, interactive tools, alerts, and other resources that help you learn about investing and how to protect yourself from financial mistakes and fraud.

Want to get better control of the stuff in your life? A professional organizer just might be the answer for you. Organized people may save time and money, with an added bonus of less stress. Read organization success stories and find a professional at the National Association of Professional Organizers website **(www. napo.net).**

Uncle Sam : The Gnome in the Know
The Government Can Help, Too

People say you must really be living in a fairy tale if you think that the government can be helpful, but these agencies actually provide consumer-friendly websites and other good information.

Financial Planning Tools
www.mymoney.gov

The content of this United States government website is organized into the categories, "Life Events," "My Resources," and "Tools." Be prepared to discover where you are in life, who you are, and the tools to help you achieve a new level of understanding.

Estimate Your Social Security
www.socialsecurity.gov

Estimated Social Security benefits can be an important part of your retirement plan. Visit the Social Security website to estimate your benefits and download helpful publications. When you are ready to retire, or if you become disabled or are a surviving spouse, you can apply online for benefits.

Tax and Retirement Information
www.irs.gov

When you visit this website, click on the tab for "Individual." Here, you will find links to frequently asked questions and various other functions, such as how to order a copy of your tax return. You can also file your income tax return for free. The website provides step-by-step instructions and a helpful video. This is an excellent tool as long as you do not need tax planning. The IRS website also has pages designed specifically for the self-employed, business owners, and other entities.

Health Help
www.healthfinder.gov

Good health is a huge part of your financial plan. Take care of yourself and help avoid medical expenses, if possible. The Health Finder website provides information about health plan options as well as prevention and wellness. The "Popular Request" tab lets you know what other people are asking about, and what maybe you should be clued in on, too.

Federal Citizens Information Center
www.pueblo.gsa.gov

Everything that you always wanted to know but were afraid to ask could be the motto of this government site. It touts itself as the easy way to get information and order consumer publications. It also offers online tips and guides. Subscribe to the free consumer information quarterly catalog or get online tips from a plethora of other government sites. Educators and speakers can order publications for their classroom or presentations.

ABOUT THE AUTHORS

Both Christine and Renee share a zeal for Helping people, especially women, make financial decisions with confidence. Both have earned the Certified Financial Planner™ professional designation and have, collectively, over fifty years of experience.

In 2008 Christine and Renee cofounded the not-for-profit Savvy Women Advice Network, Inc. (SWAN), and began facilitating discussions on a wide range of financial topics. In 2009 they began telling financial fables in effort to keep these discussions fresh and fun. In 2010, they recognized they could reach so many more people if they wrote a book. So they began collecting and refining their favorite financial fables and transformation tips.

Finally, in 2012 *Financial Fables: Seven Tales to Transform your Financial Life and More* was published. They hope individuals, as well as professionals, will find their book an enjoyable way to keep financial conversations fun and keep the networking going.

Christine C. Cargnoni, MBA, CFP® Professional

Christine is a businesswoman, educator, speaker, author, and a life coach to a wide circle of friends. She has a passion for the emerging fields of financial psychology, economic behavior, and the holistic study of money and self.

Christine is the Managing Director of L.I.F.E. (Leveraged Individual Financial Education) Services, LLC, a financial education company based in Naples, Florida. The mission of the company is to help people achieve their own personal success with the proper financial tools available to them. The company motto is – leverage what you know to a higher plateau. She is equipped to speak on a range of topics to groups and at conferences. As an award winner in the Toastmasters International division, she has the ability to share challenging concepts in an understandable, engaging manner. She also provides financial education to individuals who need to get started in the right direction and stay on course.

Education:
BA, University of Pittsburgh
MBA, Nova Southeastern University

Renee M. Porter-Medley, CFP® Practitioner

Renee is a keen observer of life and financial lessons to be learned. She is a wife, mother, and sister to seven siblings. With three daughters, a grandson and twenty four nieces and nephews, she is especially committed to helping the next generation transform their financial lives and more.

Renee has been a Certified Financial Planner practitioner for twenty-five years and advises a wide range of clients. She specializes in planning for retirement, business succession planning, and philanthropic counsel. She has taught numerous workshops and authored a variety of articles. In addition, Renee is recognized as a Qualified Kingdom Advisor which equips her to share Biblical wisdom with clients who would like to integrate their faith into their decision making process. Faith, family and extensive experience contribute to Renee's success as a trusted advisor.

Education:
BA, the University of Michigan at Dearborn
FPA Residency Program at DePaul University

Other Resources Provided by Christine and Renee

Would you like to use *Financial Fables* for a discussion group, book club, or presentation?
We provide everything you need for a Financial Storytelling™ presentation or to facilitate a discussion group. This includes a presenter or facilitator's outline that corresponds to a participant's handout and provides the Transformation Tips and Resources specific to the Financial Fable being discussed.

Learn more by visiting **www.financialstorytelling.com**, or
E-mail us at **admin@financialstorytelling.com**

Additional copies of *Financial Fables* can be purchased at **www.amazon.com**

Need a speaker for your next event?
L.I.F.E. speakers cover a wide range of topics that appeal to diverse audiences, but, of course, talks that include financial fables are of particular interest. L.I.F.E. Managing Director Christine Cargnoni is a member and a former area governor of Toastmasters International. She especially enjoys giving talks that include whimsy, humor, or wit.

Learn more at **www.financeinlife.com.**

ACKNOWLEDGMENTS

We would to thank all the women who participated in our Savvy Women Advice Network (SWAN) discussion groups. Your enthusiastic response to our financial fables and the lessons you learned encouraged us to gather them together in this book.

We would also like to thank our families for their support. You allowed us to carve out precious time from our busy family lives to write this book.

www.ingramcontent.com/pod-product-compliance
Lightning Source LLC
Chambersburg PA
CBHW022020170526
45157CB00003B/1308

978145636097 9